CHOP, COOK, YÚM!

First published 2022 by The O'Brien Press Ltd,
12 Terenure Road East, Rathgar, D06 HD27, Dublin 6, Ireland.
Tel: +353 1 4923333; Fax: +353 1 4922777
E-mail: books@obrien.ie
Website: obrien.ie
The O'Brien Press is a member of Publishing Ireland.

ISBN: 978-1-78849-274-4

Disclaimer
The publisher and author are not liable for any loss or injury resulting from these
recipes and/or use of kitchen utensils and/or cooking equipment. Children
should be supervised in the kitchen at all times.

Published in

DUBLIN
UNESCO
City of Literature

CHOP, COOK, YUM!

RECIPES FROM THE COOL FOOD SCHOOL

DEIRDRE DOYLE

THE O'BRIEN PRESS
DUBLIN

Contents

Introduction

Hi there and welcome to my kitchen!

Deirdre here from The Cool Food School. I'm a mum of three and I've been teaching food education and cooking to children in schools, at events and online since 2018.

I think food is amazing: all the different tastes, flavours and spices that are available to us, how things grow, where food comes from, the many ways to cook it and enjoy it. I love sharing my passion for food with you and having fun with it.

All the recipes in this book can be cooked by young chefs: we'll let you know if there's a bit where you need to call in an adult. Feel free to mess around with the recipes and come up with your own versions – these recipes are meant as a guide only and to help you get started.

Above all, have fun cooking. Whack your favourite songs on, have a bit of a dance around the kitchen and, best of all, eat what you make!

Deirdre

Meet the Kitchen Gang

You'll find Ollie, Molly or Chuck above every recipe. Look for the character that's closest to your age at the top of each page to find the recipes most suitable for you to make!

 Chuck is six years and four months old. His recipes are ones that everyone from the age of six can make.

 Molly is eight years and eleven months old. Her recipes are a little bit more difficult than Chuck's, but easier than Ollie's.

 Ollie is ten years and nine months old. His recipes are the trickiest.

How To Use This Book

As well as having Ollie, Molly and Chuck to help you decide if you're old enough to make a recipe, there are extra symbols in the book:

1. This symbol means you have to take extra care with the recipe, because you may be using a knife or grater, cooking on a hot stove, or using the oven. You should get an adult to help you with these tasks.

Each recipe has the following information:

2. This tells you how long it will take to get everything ready.

3. This is how long to cook the dish for.

4. This shows the number of people the recipe will feed (approximately).

5. Stuff you'll need is a list of the tools you'll need: bowls, spoons, tins, etc.

6. Food you'll need is a list of the ingredients used in the recipe.

Look out for Cool Food Facts and Fun, Cool Food Tips and Kitchen Challenges!

Stuff You'll Need and How To Use It

Every chef, big or small, needs some equipment to get started. When you're making one of the recipes, check to make sure you have all the equipment you need before you start. Take it out of the cupboard or drawer and have it ready to go.

Chopping board: Always use a chopping board when you are cutting things, rather than the counter or table, as you could damage them and your knife. Put a wet piece of kitchen paper or tea towel under the chopping board (make sure you wring out any extra wetness!) to keep the chopping board from sliding all over the place.

Blender (food processor): A blender makes some recipes very easy and cuts down on chopping time. Some recipes can't be made without a blender, like smoothies or hummus. Always lift the blade out before you pour out the contents of your blender. You might need an adult to help with this. And always keep the lid on when you're blending (it will be very messy otherwise!).

Child-safe peeler: Use a safe peeler. Make sure to peel away from your hand so you don't peel your fingers!

Grater: When you're grating, a good tip is not to grate the food all the way to the end because then you might grate your fingers too! Pop that small bit of cheese or carrot into your mouth as a reward for all your hard work and as a way to save your knuckles!

Measuring cups and spoons: Using measuring cups and spoons is far easier than using weighing scales. If you don't have measuring cups, then use a normal teacup (not a massive mug) instead. Make sure to use the same one the whole time or your recipe will not be right! For measuring spoons, you can use a normal teaspoon in your cutlery drawer.

Three teaspoons equal one tablespoon.

Child-safe knife: Make sure you have a knife suitable for your age and ability. Here are two safe ways to cut with your knife:

The Claw Hold your knife securely in one hand and curl the fingers of your other hand into a claw. Use your claw to hold tight to one end of the ingredient you're chopping. Now you can chop the food and use your knuckles to guide the knife. Your fingers are tucked safely away in your claw!

The Bridge Hold the food item with your thumb on one side and your index or pointer finger on the other side, making a bridge over the piece of food. This holds it in place so you can safely cut through it.

Staying Safe in the Kitchen

The kitchen can be a dangerous place, with hot ovens, hot cookers, sharp knives and dancing children! Here are a few rules you should always follow:

- Always have an adult around when you cook, especially when there is heat involved. Make sure adults help with the dangerous jobs! You'll see them marked with this symbol: 🖐
- If you have long hair, tie it up – who wants a hair in their dinner? Roll up your sleeves so they don't dangle in the food, and wear an apron to keep you clean and tidy.
- Wash your hands before cooking. Wash them during cooking too, like when you use raw chicken or do something messy, and always wash them after you've finished cooking.
- Don't run in the kitchen. Kitchens can get messy and dirty and the floor can be slippy so you might fall if you run.
- Clean up spills as soon as they happen. This helps to prevent accidents and makes cleaning up easier.
- When using saucepans on the cooker, always turn the handle to the side away from the edge so it's not poking out. This will stop the saucepan from going flying if someone knocks into it.
- Always switch the cooker and the oven off when you're finished cooking.
- Wear oven gloves when taking hot trays or dishes out of the oven.
- When using raw meat or chicken, always wash your hands, board and knife straight afterwards so you don't poison anyone!
- Make sure to check the ingredients list to see if you're allergic to anything, and if you're sharing food with friends, let them know what's in there. And don't bring nuts (or sesame seeds) to school.

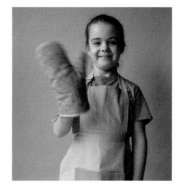

Clean Up

It is very important to clean up the kitchen when you're finished cooking. Here's why:

- If you don't clean up, the adults will be mad and you won't be allowed to cook again!
- If you leave out ingredients like milk or cheese, they will go off. Put them away as soon as you're finished with them.
- It's not very comfortable to eat in a messy kitchen so clean up as you go and then give the kitchen a final clean when you're finished cooking.
- Everyone who cooks should help to clean up. It's boring but has to be done. Try our kitchen challenge to get it done quickly.

Kitchen Challenge

When it's time to clean up, pick your favourite song or take it in turns to pick the tunes and try and get all the cleaning up done by the time your song is over!

Or put the names of all the jobs on scraps of paper - like 'load the dishwasher', 'sweep the floor', 'wipe down the counter' - and take it in turns to pick out the jobs. Leave one scrap of paper blank so whoever gets that one can relax!

Top Tips for Cooking

1. Cracking eggs

Tap the egg gently against the side of the bowl or on the countertop until you have a crack. Then, holding the egg over the bowl, use your thumbs to pull the shell apart. In plops the egg. If some shell falls in, use a larger bit of the shell or a wet finger to get it out.

2. Checking your baking is done

To make sure bread or muffins are fully baked, carefully take them out of the oven using oven gloves, or get an adult to help. Take a clean knife, push it into the middle of the loaf, or the middle of the biggest muffin, and pull it out. If it's clean, your baking is ready. If there's goo on the knife, it needs to go back in for a few more minutes.

3. Knowing when chicken is cooked

This is kinda important as uncooked chicken can make you sick. Carefully remove a large piece of chicken from the pot or tray. On your chopping board, cut into the thickest part of the chicken. If it's white all the way through, it's good to go. If it's still a bit pink inside, it needs more cooking time.

4. Cutting an avocado

The best way to cut an avocado is to push the tip of your knife into the top of the avocado and push it into the middle until it can't go any further. It has met the stone! Then, keeping your knife touching the stone, twist the avocado until the skin is cut all the way around. Remove the knife and twist the avocado – et voilà, your avocado should open!

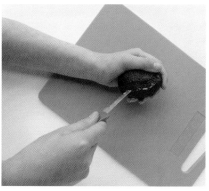

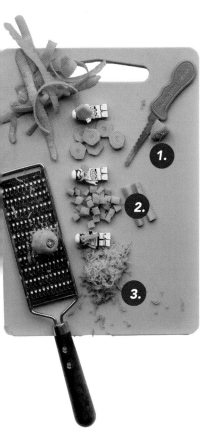

 **5. How to chop food**

There are lots of different ways to chop food:

1. Slice This is cutting your veggies into nice even slices. They take longer to cook when sliced but they are great this way when you're serving them raw with hummus or pesto.

2. Dice This is when you cut the food into small, even cubes or pieces. They will cook evenly and look better! Used in lots of dishes like soup and tomato sauce.

3. Grate This is when you use the grater to make your veggies really small. Grated veggies cook the quickest. They are also nice to eat raw – grated carrot in your tuna mix, for example.

6. How to grease a dish

It's important to grease your dish when you're baking something so that it doesn't stick. Take a piece of kitchen paper and pour a capful of oil onto it, or use a knob of butter on some greaseproof paper, and wipe all around the inside of the tin or muffin tray.

7. Coating a pan with oil

When frying food, it's important that the whole pan is covered in oil to stop the food from sticking. Pour some oil on your pan and then tilt the pan around until the oil covers the bottom.

8. Turning on the oven first

Turn the oven on before you're ready to pop whatever you're making into it. This is because it takes a little while for your oven to reach the right temperature. If the oven is not warm when you put the food in, then you'll either have to cook it for longer or it won't cook properly at all.

9. Melting chocolate

There are a number of recipes in the book that use melted chocolate. You can melt chocolate in two ways:

- In the microwave: put the chocolate into the microwave in a suitable bowl (not a metal one). Microwave for 30 seconds, take out and stir. Repeat this until the chocolate is fully melted. Don't leave it in for too long at a time as the chocolate will burn. Be careful taking it out as the bowl will be hot!

- In a 'bain-marie': get two bowls or a bowl and a saucepan. Carefully pour some boiling water into the saucepan or bottom bowl and sit the other bowl on top. Stir the chocolate until it's melted. This lets the chocolate melt slowly so it doesn't burn.

Don't forget to lick the spoon when you're finished!

10. Presenting your food

Try to make your food look nice and fancy when you're putting it on the plate. Think of how you might get it in a restaurant.

- Make sure the plate is clean.
- Arrange the food to look as nice as you can.
- Use chopped-up fresh herbs to decorate your plate (for dinners and snacks) or berries and a sprinkle of cinnamon (for sweet dishes).

Now let's get cooking!

Morning Munchies

Vanilla Porridge

Porridge is made from oats, which grow very easily in Ireland – they like all the rain we get!

 2 mins   5–6 minutes   1 adult or 2 children

Stuff you'll need
a biggish bowl
spoon

Food you'll need
½ cup oats
1½ cups milk or milk and water mixed
1 tsp vanilla extract
2 tsp chia seeds

How to make it
1 Put all the ingredients into a biggish bowl and mix everything well.
2 Pop the bowl into the microwave on high for 2 minutes.
3 Take it out and stir it, then put it back in for another 30 seconds. Careful, as the bowl will be hot!
4 Take it out and stir again, and microwave it again for another 30 seconds.
5 Keep doing this until it is nice and thick and creamy and yummy! Let it sit for a minute to thicken up, then top it with some tasty toppings!

Try these tasty toppings

- chia seed jam (see page 34)
- chocolate chips
- flaked almonds or chopped toasted walnuts (for how to toast nuts, see page 27)
- honey or maple syrup
- raisins
- desiccated coconut
- pumpkin seeds or sunflower seeds
- fresh fruit

Porridge Cake

Everyone dreams of having cake for breakfast. Well, now you can with this brilliant recipe!

 5–10 minutes (prepare it the night before and store in the fridge)

 35–40 minutes

 3 children and 2 adults

Stuff you'll need

chopping board
child-safe knife
baking dish (10 x 8" approx.)
small bowl

measuring cups
fork
big bowl

Food you'll need

2 ripe bananas
2 eggs
2 cups milk of choice
1 tsp vanilla extract
3 cups oats
1 tbsp chia seeds
1 cup frozen berries (e.g. raspberries)

Optional extras
1 tbsp desiccated coconut
1 tbsp chopped nuts of choice
1 tbsp choc chips
2 tbsp cacao powder (for chocolate porridge cake!)

To serve: crème fraîche and fresh fruit

How to make it

1 Turn on your oven to 180 degrees.
 2 Slice the bananas and spread them evenly on the bottom of your baking dish.
3 In a small bowl, mix the egg, milk and vanilla together (wet ingredients).
4 In a big bowl, add the oats and chia seeds (dry ingredients) and any optional extras you fancy.
5 Mix the wet and dry ingredients together. It should be quite runny (add some more milk if it's not).
6 Pour this over the banana slices, making sure they are completely covered.
7 Scatter some frozen berries on top.
8 Bake for 35–40 minutes at 180 degrees.
 9 Carefully take it out of the oven and serve straightaway with some crème fraîche and fresh fruit – yum!

Easy-peasy Oaty Bread

Use the tub from your yoghurt to measure the porridge oats!

 10 minutes

45–55 minutes

3 children and 2 adults for lunch or breakfast

Stuff you'll need

loaf tin

baking paper

large bowl

measuring spoons

small bowl

whisk

Food you'll need

1 x 500g tub natural yoghurt

2 tubs oats (or 370g)

2 tsp bicarbonate of soda (or baking soda)

pinch of salt

handful of seeds (e.g. sunflower)

3–4 tbsp milk

1 egg

small handful of sesame seeds for decoration

How to make it

1 Turn the oven on to 180 degrees.

2 Grease a loaf tin (see how on page 13) and line it with baking paper.

3 Plop your yoghurt into a large bowl.

4 Using the empty tub from your yoghurt, fill it twice with oats and dump them on top of the yoghurt.

5 Add the bicarbonate of soda, salt and seeds to the large bowl and mix well.

6 Whisk the milk and egg together in a small bowl, and then add to the large bowl.

7 Mix everything together until all the oats are coated in yoghurt.

8 Pour into the loaf tin, smooth with the back of a spoon, and scatter the sesame seeds over the top.

9 Pop into the oven for about 45–55 minutes or until a knife inserted into the middle comes out clean.

10 If you want a really crispy crust, take the bread out of the loaf tin and return it to the oven, directly on the rack, for a further 5 minutes.

11 Leave it to cool before cutting it – otherwise it will go all crumbly. Yummy with butter and cheese or chia seed jam (see page 34)!

Lazy Porridge

These are porridge oats that you leave in the fridge overnight soaking in a liquid like milk or apple juice - this softens the oats so you don't have to cook them in the morning and you can stay in bed longer!

 5 minutes

 (soak time) overnight in the fridge

 1 or 2 children

Stuff you'll need
measuring cups
spoon
airtight container

Food you'll need
1 cup oats
1 cup milk of your choice (cow's, oat, coconut, almond, etc.)
1 tbsp chia seeds
2 tsp maple syrup
1 tsp vanilla extract
toppings (see below for suggestions)

How to make it
1 Put all the ingredients into the airtight container and mix everything really well together.
2 Put the lid on the container and pop it into the fridge before you head to bed.
3 In the morning, top with any (or all) of the following: toasted almonds*, toasted pumpkin or sunflower seeds*, berries, such as blueberries, strawberries or raspberries, Greek yoghurt, banana and honey, cocoa powder, chocolate chips, peanut or almond butter, coconut.

* See page 27 for how to toast nuts and seeds.

Try these tasty toppings
- blueberries, banana and honey
- toasted flaked almonds and berries
- a little bit of everything!

Scrummy Scrambled Eggs

This easy-peasy breakfast will keep you full for hours afterwards because of all the protein in the eggs.

 2 minutes

 about 3–5 minutes

 1 or 2 children

Stuff you'll need

bowl

measuring spoon

fork

small saucepan

wooden spoon

child-safe knife

Food you'll need per person

2 eggs

1 tbsp milk

2 slices wholemeal bread

1 tsp butter

How to make it

1 Carefully crack the eggs into the bowl (see page 12 for how to crack eggs).

2 Add the milk and whisk everything together.

3 Put your bread into the toaster.

 4 Melt the butter in the saucepan and when it's melted, pour in the eggs.

5 Let them cook for about 30 seconds or until the bottom of the eggs is solid. Gently stir with your wooden spoon once and leave to cook again.

6 After another 30 seconds or when the eggs are nearly all solid, take the saucepan off the cooker. They will keep cooking in the warm pan. Stir gently.

7 When your toast has popped, butter it and cut it into quarters if you like. Serve immediately with your eggs on top or on the side!

Things that are nice to eat with scrambled eggs

- chopped tomato
- slices of avocado
- a sprinkling of grated cheddar cheese
- beans (see page 74)
- smoked salmon

Bestest Banana Pancakes

These are the easiest and bestest pancakes to make and they have only two ingredients!

 2 minutes

 5 minutes

 1 or 2 children

Stuff you'll need
plate
potato masher or fork
bowl
fork
frying pan
spoon
spatula or fish slice

Food you'll need
1 medium banana
1 egg
butter for frying

To serve:
natural yoghurt
raspberries
toasted chopped nuts

How to make it
1 Mash the banana on a plate.
2 Crack the egg into a bowl, add the mashed banana and mix well until it's all well combined.
 3 Melt some butter in a frying pan.
4 Spoon out tablespoons of the mixture onto the pan to make smallish pancakes (they'll be easier to flip if they're small!).
 5 Fry gently for a minute or so and when the bottom is solid, flip it onto the other side with your spatula or fish slice and cook for a further minute or so.
6 Serve straight away, topped with natural yoghurt, mushed-up raspberries and toasted nuts.

Toasted nuts and seeds
Turn the oven on to 180 degrees. Scatter raw nuts or seeds on a baking tray, making sure they all have plenty of room. Toast for 5–15 minutes, depending on the size of the nuts. Keep checking them so they don't burn!

Gorgeous Granola

Granola is toasted oats with nuts, seeds and fruit, oil to stick everything together and a sweetener like honey. Delicious!

 About 10 minutes

 20 minutes

 2 adults and 3 children for 2–3 days

Stuff you'll need

measuring cups

chopping board

child-safe knife

large bowl

small, non-metal bowl

baking tray

spoon

Food you'll need

1 cup mixed nuts and seeds (sunflower seeds, pumpkin seeds, cashew nuts, pecans, peanuts, sliced almonds)

4 cups oats

½ cup coconut oil

½ cup maple syrup or honey

1 tsp cinnamon

1 tbsp desiccated coconut

½ cup dried fruit (raisins, apricots, etc.)

½ cup dark chocolate chips

How to make it

1 Turn your oven on to 180 degrees.

2 Roughly chop the nuts.

3 Add the oats to a large bowl.

4 Measure out the coconut oil into a non-metal bowl and melt it in the microwave (this will take about 1 minute – you don't want it boiling!)

5 Add the melted coconut oil and maple syrup or honey to the bowl and mix well. Make sure all the oats are coated. Add the cinnamon, chopped nuts and seeds. Mix everything really well.

6 Line a large baking tray with baking paper and tip the mixture onto the tray.

7 Spread it evenly over the tray and press it down firmly with the back of a spoon.

8 Pop it into the oven for 20 minutes, mixing it after the first 10 minutes.

9 Take the tray out of the oven and sprinkle the coconut on top.

 10 Return to the oven for another 5 minutes.

 11 Remove and press the hot granola down with the back of a spoon to help form clumps.

12 Let it cool completely – no sneaky tasting or you'll burn your tongue!

13 Break it up with your hands. Add the dried fruit and chocolate chips and mix everything together.

14 Store the granola in an airtight jar for up to a month. Add milk for an easy breakfast or have it dry as a snack!

**Crazy Carrot
Cocktail**

**Green Slime
Delight**

**Purple Pee
Surprise**

How Do You Smoothie?

Smoothies can be a healthy snack or a quick breakfast but it's important to always include a vegetable like spinach as well as proteins and healthy fats. This helps to keep you fuller for longer and gives you energy for running and playing!

 5 minutes

 5–10 minutes

 1 or 2 children

Stuff you'll need

peeler

child-safe knife

chopping board

blender

a glass

How to make it

 Blend everything together until smooth, adding extra water or ice to taste.

Crazy Carrot Cocktail

Food you'll need

2 whole oranges (peeled)

1 carrot (peeled and quartered)

1 banana

½ avocado

Green Slime Delight

Food you'll need

4–5 fresh or frozen strawberries

1 cup natural yoghurt

small handful spinach leaves

vanilla extract

1 tbsp cashews

Purple Pee Surprise

Food you'll need

2 whole oranges (peeled)

1 beetroot (cooked)

1 cup frozen berries

1 apple (chopped)

1 tsp chia seeds

Cool Food Fact

Eating beetroot may turn your pee pink - but you'll have to try it to see (that's the surprise)!

Smoothie Planner

Create your own smoothie!

1. Pick one cup chopped fruit

apple, strawberries, watermelon, blueberries, banana, pineapple, grapes, pear, kiwi, raspberries, orange, mango

2. Pick one vegetable

cup of spinach/kale
¼ cucumber
1 stalk celery
1 cooked beetroot
½ carrot
½ cup broccoli

3. Pick a liquid (1–2 cups)

water
milk
coconut milk
almond/soya milk
beetroot juice
fresh orange juice

How to make it

1 Pick something from columns 1, 2 and 3.
2 Add items from columns 4 and 5 to taste. Blitz.
3 Add more liquid for a thinner smoothie and ice to cool it.
4 Experiment and have fun!
5 Leftovers can be frozen to make smoothie pops!

4. Pick one healthy fat

½ avocado
3–4 raw cashews
2–3 raw walnuts
5–10 raw almonds
1 tbsp nut butter
1 tbsp coconut oil
1 tbsp chia seeds
1 tbsp flax seeds (ground)
1 tbsp Udo's Oil®

5. A little something extra

1 tbsp live natural yoghurt
1 tsp honey
1–2 tbsp raw oats
1 tsp vanilla extract
raw cacao powder*
¼ inch ginger root
1 tbsp fresh mint

* This is what chocolate is made from!

Chia Seed Jam

If you grow your own berries, this is a great way to use them up before the birds eat them. Frozen berries work great too!

 5 minutes

 5 minutes

 1 medium jar

Stuff you'll need

measuring cups and spoons

small saucepan

wooden spoon

1 airtight jar

Food you'll need

2 cups fresh or frozen raspberries

1 tbsp maple syrup

1 tsp vanilla extract

2 tbsp chia seeds

How to make it

1 Tip your raspberries into the saucepan and cook on a low heat for about 5 minutes until they have gone all mushy (don't they smell delicious?).

2 Add a teaspoon or two of water if the raspberries are sticking.

3 Add the maple syrup and vanilla and cook for a further minute or so.

4 Add the chia seeds and cook for another 5 minutes on a low heat. Add water if the jam is starting to stick.

5 Let it cool and then spoon it into a clean, clear airtight jar. It will keep in the fridge for about a week (if it lasts that long!).

Cool Food Fact

Chia seeds are an ancient food from South America and are full of fibre (which is great for helping us poo) and protein. They soak up to about ten times their weight in liquid and turn into a gel so they are great for making jam!

Eat the

In Ireland we talk about finding the pot of gold at the end of the rainbow. By eating the rainbow, your pot of gold will be filled with superpowers like strong bones, a good memory and energy to play and dance.

Red
Red apples
Red peppers
Strawberries
Tomatoes
Watermelon
Good for your heart and your memory

Yellow
Bananas
Lemons
Pineapple
Yellow peppers
Good for your heart and skin and for healing wounds

Purple and blue
Aubergines
Beetroot
Blueberries
Purple grapes
Red cabbage
Good for your memory and keeping you strong

Rainbow

Green
Broccoli
Green apples
Green beans
Kiwi fruit
Lettuce
Peas
Sugar snap peas
Good for strong bones

Orange
Carrots
Mango
Melon
Oranges
Orange peppers
Sweet potatoes
Good for keeping you strong and well

Cool Rainbow Challenge
Have a rainbow week! Pick a colour each day and eat as many foods of that colour as you can, e.g. orange - orange smoothie for breakfast, carrot sticks for lunch, sweet potatoes for dinner.

Tasty Toast Toppers

Toast is an easy-peasy breakfast to make. You can use lots of different types of bread but especially yummy is the oaty bread from page 20. Then pick your favourite topping!

🔪 5 minutes

⏱ 5 minutes

How to make it

Toast your bread and then pick any one of the toppers below. Don't forget to include some protein for those muscles and for keeping you full!

Peanut butter with blueberries and chocolate chips

Peanut butter with chia seed jam

Peanut butter with raisins and banana

Boiled egg with tomato

Scrambled egg with avocado butter

Hummus with cheese

Avocado with tomatoes and toasted seeds (see page 27 for how to toast seeds)

Cream cheese with chia seed jam (see page 34 for how to make chia seed jam)

Cheddar cheese with banana

Mozzarella with tomato

Lunchbox Fillers

All About Sandwiches

Sandwiches are the easiest thing to pop into your lunchbox.
A sandwich has two main ingredients: bread and fillings.

Bread

Try different breads in your lunchbox – here are some suggestions:

baguette	sourdough bread
ciabatta	spelt bread
Easy-peasy Oaty Bread (see page 20)	wholemeal bagel
roll	wholemeal bread
rye bread	wholemeal pitta
soda bread	wholemeal wrap

What's with all the wholemeal breads?

Wholemeal means that the bakery has used the whole grain from the wheat, including the bran and the germ. It is higher in fibre and helps you poo better! If you're not keen on wholemeal bread, try making your sandwich with one slice of white bread and one of wholemeal.

Fillings

Turkey

- leftover sliced turkey with cheddar cheese and rocket leaves
- diced turkey with mayo and cucumber

Cheese

- cheddar cheese with apple slices and lettuce
- cream cheese with grated carrot

Egg

- Egg mayonnaise – peel and mash your hard-boiled eggs. Add in some mayo and chopped spring onion. Mix well.
- sliced boiled egg and lettuce.

Chicken

- leftover sliced roast chicken with iceberg lettuce and mayonnaise
- cooked chicken with mashed avocado, sliced peppers and cheese in a wrap
- chicken and sweetcorn mayonnaise with lettuce
- Totally Tasty Chicken wrap (see page 47)

Tuna

- tuna with mayonnaise (or Greek yoghurt) and any of the following: grated carrot, sweetcorn, diced cucumber, diced onion, diced celery or chopped grapes. (If you don't like tuna, try mashed chickpeas.)

(Don't use tomatoes in your sandwiches: they make them all soggy!)

Other Bits and Pieces for Your Lunchbox

- Raw veggies – sugar snap peas (listen to them pop when you break them!), carrot, cucumber, cherry tomatoes, pepper slices, radish
- Cooked veggies like corn on the cob, carrots, broccoli, cauliflower with a dip
- Yoghurt – choose natural yoghurt or Greek yoghurt and add your own fruit
- Fruit selection (apple, pear, orange, banana, sliced melon, blueberries, kiwi, grapes, raspberries, strawberries)
- Oatcakes
- Wholemeal crackers
- Hummus
- Popcorn
- Pretzels
- Tomato Pinwheels (see page 73)
- Chia seed jam (see page 34)
- Hard-boiled egg
- Banana Sushi (see page 51)
- Porridge Cake (see page 19)
- Leftover pancakes
- Egg muffins (see page 44)
- Power balls (see page 55)
- Cheese slices or cubes
- Meat slices (beef, chicken, ham, turkey)
- Leftover dinner like pasta, frittata, pizza
- Wholemeal pasta, plain or mixed with diced peppers, cucumber and mayonnaise
- Dry wholegrain cereal like Shreddies®
- Quinoa or rice
- Soup (in a flask)
- Nut-free smoothie (remember: don't bring any nuts to school as someone might be allergic!)

Hummus Atā Tū?

Hummus is sooo handy. You can put it on your sandwiches or have it as a dip with veggies or just eat it with a spoon!

 5 minutes 5 minutes 6–8 servings

Stuff you'll need

measuring spoons
blender
child-safe knife

Food you'll need

1 clove of garlic
1 can of chickpeas
2 tbsp tahini*
1 tsp ground cumin

juice of 1 lemon
4 tbsp olive oil
salt, to taste

* You can leave this out if there are allergies to sesame seeds in your class or family.

How to make it

1 Peel the garlic by squashing the clove with the heel of your hand to release the skin.
2 Add it and the chickpeas, tahini and ground cumin to the blender.
 3 Cut the lemon in half and squeeze the juice into the blender as well.
4 Add a couple of tablespoons of olive oil to start.
 5 Turn on the blender and let it work its magic! Add the rest of the oil slowly.
6 Blend everything until it's smooth. You may have to stop the blender, scrape the mixture down off the sides and blend again. Taste it to see if it needs more cumin, lemon juice or salt.
7 Serve with carrot, pepper and cucumber sticks or try a hummus and cheese sandwich!
8 This hummus will keep in the fridge for 3 to 5 days.

Try these tasty options

Add a tablespoon of roasted red peppers or 1 small cooked beetroot to your hummus to make it crazy deliciouser!

Spinach and Cheese Egg Muffin Thingies

These will keep for a couple of days in the fridge and are great lunchbox fillers!

 5–10 minutes   about 15 minutes   makes 12 muffins

Stuff you'll need
chopping board
child-safe knife
jug
whisk or fork
muffin tray
cooling rack

Food you'll need
1 cup of spinach leaves
6 cherry tomatoes
8 eggs
salt and pepper
1 cup of grated cheddar cheese

How to make it
1 Turn on the oven to 180 degrees.
 2 Roll the spinach into a ball and chop it up using the claw hold (see page 9).
 3 Cut the cherry tomatoes in half.
4 Whisk the eggs together in a jug and add a pinch of salt and pepper.
5 Grease your muffin tray (see how on page 13).
6 Divide the chopped spinach between the 12 muffin cups.
7 Add some grated cheese to each muffin cup.
8 Pour the egg mixture slowly (this can get messy!) on top of the cheese.
9 Plop half a cherry tomato on top of each muffin thingy, cut side up.
10 Bake in the oven for 12–15 minutes until the egg is completely cooked.
 11 Take them carefully out of the oven and cool on a cooling rack. Eat them warm from the oven (best) or let them cool down and pop some into your lunchbox.

Top Tip
Instead of cheese and spinach, try other options like mushrooms and peas (pictured), ham and cheese or chicken and peppers.

Totally Tasty Chicken Wrap

This is a really yummy filling for a wrap or you can use it in whatever bread you fancy.

 about 15 minutes

 about 10 minutes

 3 children

Stuff you'll need

small saucepan
chopping board
child-safe knife
bowl
measuring spoons

Food you'll need

2 free-range chicken breasts
handful of red grapes
handful of rocket leaves
1 tbsp mayonnaise
1 tsp curry powder
3 wholemeal wraps

How to make it

1 Pop the chicken breasts into the saucepan and cover them with cold water.

 2 Bring them to the boil and then turn down the heat. Let them cook for 12–15 minutes – you'll know the chicken is cooked if you cut into it and it's white all the way through (see the tip on page 12).

 3 When the chicken is done, take it out of the water and let it cool.

 4 While the chicken is cooling, rinse the grapes and chop them in quarters.

 5 Bunch the rocket together on your chopping board and cut it into smaller pieces using the claw hold (see page 9).

 6 When the chicken is cold, chop it into small pieces and throw it into a largish bowl.

7 Add the rocket and grapes, the mayonnaise and the curry powder. Give everything a good mix. Add more mayonnaise if needed.

8 Take your wraps and spread a couple of spoonfuls of the mixture into the middle.

 9 Roll them up and cut them in half. Put them in your lunchbox – they will keep you going all day in school!

Waterford Tuna Blaa

Tuna is a great filling for sandwiches. It has got lots of protein which helps your muscles grow and keeps your tummy full.

🔪 about 5 minutes

🍽️ 3 children

Stuff you'll need

tin opener
bowl
spoon
chopping board
child-safe knife

Food you'll need

2 tbsp frozen sweetcorn
1 x 145g tin tuna (sustainably caught)
1–2 tbsp mayonnaise
3 Waterford blaas (soft white bread
    rolls) or wholemeal bread/wraps
lettuce

How to make it

 1 Put the sweetcorn into a bowl with a tablespoon of water and microwave it on medium for 3–4 minutes. Allow it to cool.

2 Open the tin of tuna and drain off the liquid, using the lid to hold the fish in place.

3 Plop the tuna into a bowl and add the sweetcorn and mayonnaise. Mix really well.

 4 Cut each blaa in two and butter it if you like. Spread some of the tuna mixture onto one half.

5 Add some lettuce. Pop the top of the blaa on and cut in two.

6 Pack it into your lunchbox along with some fruit and veggies for a great lunch!

Snackalicious

twenty-four

2×10

5×4

6×2

Bonkers-easy Banana Sushi

Here are two great fun ways to make this dish. If you don't fancy peanut butter, try cream cheese instead!

🥖 2 minutes

🍲 1 or 2 children

Method 1

Stuff you'll need

chopping board
child-safe knife

Food you'll need

1 wholemeal wrap
peanut butter (smooth or crunchy, 100% natural if possible)
1 banana

How to make it

1 Lay your wholemeal wrap flat on a chopping board.

2 Spread it with lots of peanut butter.

3 Place the banana at one side of the wrap.

4 Straighten out the banana a little – it might break but that's ok!

5 Roll it up in the wrap as tight as you can.

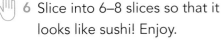 6 Slice into 6–8 slices so that it looks like sushi! Enjoy.

Method 2

Stuff you'll need

chopping board
child-safe knife
bowls

Food you'll need

1 banana
peanut butter (smooth or crunchy, 100% natural if possible)
Your choice of: chia seeds, desiccated coconut, chocolate chips, toasted seeds (see page 27 for how to toast seeds)

How to make it

 1 Slice your banana into 6–7 pieces.

2 Spread the peanut butter around the outside.

3 Roll the banana slices in the toppings of your choice.

4 Arrange them nicely on a plate, and you're done! Get as creative as you want with these – try different toppings!

Fantastic Flapjacks

These flapjacks will keep you going between meals and give you lots of energy when you're doing sport or heading out on your bike.

 10–15 minutes

 20–25 minutes

 16–20 pieces approx.

Stuff you'll need

baking tray

baking paper

small bowl (microwave safe)

plate

fork

large bowl

chopping board

child-safe knife

measuring spoons

cooling rack

Food you'll need

1 cup coconut oil

2–3 ripe bananas

1–2 cups dried fruit like dates or raisins

3 cups oats

1 cup mixed seeds (chia, pumpkin, sesame, sunflower)

½ cup dark chocolate chips

1 tsp vanilla extract

2 tbsp maple syrup

Option

50g dark chocolate

How to make it

1 Turn the oven on to 200 degrees and line a large tray with baking paper.

 2 Melt the coconut oil in a small bowl in the microwave (about 1 minute). It should be like water when it's melted!

3 Mash the bananas on a plate and add to the large bowl.

 4 Add the dried fruit to the bananas. (If using dates, chop them smaller.)

5 Add the oats, seeds, chocolate chips, vanilla and maple syrup into the bowl and pour in the coconut oil. Mix everything really well.

6 Tip the mixture onto the tray and press down well with the back of your spoon.

7 Bake for 20–25 minutes until golden brown.

 8 Carefully take the tray from the oven and let the flapjacks cool down before cutting into squares or triangles.

Option
Decorate with melted chocolate!

1 Melt your chocolate (see page 14 for how to do this).
2 Using a small spoon, take some of the melted chocolate and drip it over the flapjacks in whatever pattern you like!
3 Let the chocolate harden before cutting the flapjacks into squares.

You can pop these in your lunchbox if seeds are allowed in school or have them as an after-school snack.

Powered-up Energy Balls

These energy balls give you power or energy, exactly what you need to help you run faster, read better or jump higher.

 10 minutes   10–15 minutes   makes 10–12

Stuff you'll need
2 small bowls
measuring spoons
blender
child-safe knife
chopping board
plate

Food you'll need
1 tbsp chia seeds
4 Weetabix® or wheat biscuits
1 tbsp coconut oil
8 large pitted dates (dates with no stones)
¼ cup cacao powder (plus extra for
     rolling)
2 tbsp desiccated coconut
1 tsp cinnamon

How to make it
1 Put the chia seeds into a small bowl. Add 4 tablespoons of water to the seeds and leave to one side (watch the magic happen!).
2 Meanwhile, break your Weetabixes in two and throw them into the blender.
 3 Measure out the coconut oil into a bowl and microwave it until it's melted: about 30 seconds to 1 minute.
 4 Chop the dates in two and add them, the cacao powder, desiccated coconut and the melted coconut oil to the blender.
5 Add the chia seed mixture (it should be a gooey gel now).
 6 Blitz everything together for about 30 seconds, then scrape down the sides and blend again. Keep doing this until everything is well mixed.
7 Take small amounts in your hands. Squeeze together tightly and then roll between your two hands to form a ball. If you wet your hands first, it can stop the mixture sticking to your fingers.
8 If they are not sticking together, add another date or two and blend again as this will help everything stick together.
9 Sprinkle about a tablespoon of cacao powder onto a plate and on top of that a teaspoon of cinnamon.
10 Roll the balls in the mixture and pop in the fridge for 20 minutes before gobbling them up. These are great for your lunchbox!

Cheesy Broccoli Quesadilla

This is a very different way to eat a cheese sandwich - hot from the pan!

 about 5 minutes   about 5 minutes   2 children or 1 adult

Stuff you'll need

chopping board

child-safe knife

bowl

sieve

large frying pan

measuring cups

fish slice or spatula

Food you'll need

1 spring onion

small handful broccoli florets

2 wholemeal wraps

1 cup grated cheddar cheese

sour cream and guacamole to serve

How to make it

1 Chop the top and bottom (the hairy roots!) off the spring onion and chop it into small pieces.

2 Put the broccoli florets into a bowl, cover with water and microwave for 1–2 minutes. Carefully take it out of the microwave and drain in a sieve. Chop the florets up finely.

3 Place one wrap directly on a cold frying pan (no oil needed).

4 Scatter the onion and broccoli on the wrap and top with the grated cheese.

5 Place the second wrap on top and place a bowl or plate on it to weigh it down.

6 Turn on the heat under the pan to medium and cook for about 2–3 minutes until the wrap is browned.

7 Flip over and cook the other side for 2–3 minutes. Don't let it burn!

8 Take it out of the pan, put it on a chopping board and cut it like a pizza.

9 Serve with sour cream and guacamole.

Try these tasty options

You can add lots of different ingredients to your quesadilla. Try finely chopped spinach, tomatoes or mushrooms, mashed kidney beans or cooked salmon.

Wanna Pizza My Bagel?

Who says pizza always has to be on a pizza base? Use a bagel as your base for a quick, easy and tasty snack.

 5–10 minutes

 5 minutes

 3–4 children

Stuff you'll need

baking tray (that fits under your grill)
baking paper
measuring cups

spoon
child-safe knife
chopping board

Food you'll need

3 wholemeal bagels, pre-sliced ('cos they're too tricky to cut at home!)
1 cup tomato passata or Cleverest Tomato Sauce (see page 71)

Toppings: ham, sweetcorn, peppers, mushrooms – whatever you fancy!
2 cups grated Mozzarella cheese
dried oregano

How to make it

1 Turn your grill on to medium.
2 Place the bagel halves, cut side up, on a baking tray with baking paper on it.
3 Spread the tomato passata or sauce on each bagel half.
4 Add your favourite toppings.
5 Divide the cheese between each bagel (add more if you like it really cheesy).
6 Sprinkle a pinch of oregano on top.
 7 Pop under the preheated grill for 3–5 minutes.
8 When the cheese is melted and bubbling, they are ready to go. Be careful not to burn your mouth eating them as they will be hot!

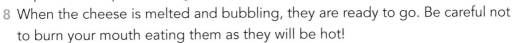

Try these tasty options
- Use wholemeal wraps instead of bagels.
- Try different toppings, like chicken and pesto or onions and tomato.

Courgette Pizza Bites

These are the easiest thing ever to make, especially if you have Cleverest Tomato Sauce knocking around your kitchen. If not, then use some pesto or passata.

 5–10 minutes

 5 minutes

 3 children for a snack

Stuff you'll need
baking tray
baking paper
child-safe knife
measuring spoons and cups
chopping board

Food you'll need
1 large courgette
1–2 tbsp Cleverest Tomato Sauce (see page 71)
½ cup grated cheese
dried oregano or basil

How to make it
1 Turn your oven on to 180 degrees.
2 Lay some baking paper on the baking tray.
3 Cut the top and bottom off your courgette.
4 Cut the courgette into thick rings and spread them on the baking tray.
5 Smear some tomato sauce on each piece of courgette.
6 Top with grated cheese.
7 Take a pinch of oregano or basil (or both!) and scatter it on the pizzas.
8 Pop them into the oven for 5–7 minutes until the cheese is bubbling.
9 Carefully take the tray from the oven and let the pizza bites cool down for a couple of minutes before devouring them!

Cool Food Tip
When a recipe asks for a pinch of something (a herb or spice normally), it's the amount you can pick up between your thumb and forefinger.

Dinky Apple Doughnuts

These are easier to make and tastier than real doughnuts! You can be really creative with them and make them look pretty or pretty crazy - you're the chef!

 5 minutes

 5–10 minutes

 2 or 3 children as a snack

Stuff you'll need

apple corer

child-safe knife

chopping board

bowl

spoon

Food you'll need

2 apples

2 tbsp cream cheese

2 tsp honey

1 tsp cinnamon

Tasty Toppings

assorted chopped nuts

raisins

chocolate chips

desiccated coconut

How to make it

1 Using an apple corer, take the middle out of the apples.

2 Slice the apples into 3 or 4 thick slices across so the slices look like doughnuts (with a hole in the middle!).

3 Mix the cream cheese with the honey and cinnamon.

4 Spread the apple slices with the cream cheese mixture.

5 Go to town topping them with whatever you fancy!

Try these tasty options
- Raisins, chocolate chips and chopped hazelnuts
- Coconut and almonds and chocolate chips
- A little bit of everything!

Totally Terrific Tomato Toasties

You can serve these with soup or as a starter at dinnertime or eat them as a snack on their own (add some cheese for protein)!

🔪 15 minutes

🍴 3 children and 2 adults as a starter or snack

Stuff you'll need
chopping board
child-safe knife
bowl

Food you'll need
8 medium tomatoes (about 500g)
4–6 tbsp extra virgin olive oil
2 tbsp balsamic vinegar
1 crusty baguette (or similar – not
  sliced pan)
1–2 garlic cloves, peeled
Handful fresh basil leaves, torn into
  small pieces

Cool Food Tip
Don't burn your toast! Have your topping ready to go as soon as it pops so that you can eat your toasties warm.

How to make it
 1 Wash and dry the tomatoes, and chop them into small pieces.

2 In a bowl, add the tomatoes, oil and vinegar.

3 Mix everything really well. Taste to see if you like it and add some salt and pepper if you like.

 4 Cut the crusty bread into thick slices.

5 Toast the bread in a toaster (or under the grill).

6 Rub the toast on one side with a peeled garlic clove.

7 Top with the tomato mixture and decorate with the basil.

8 Eat immediately!

Blurry, Flurry, Snacks in a Hurry

These snacks are great when you're starving and need something to eat NOW!

Stuff you'll need

chopping board
child-safe knife
spoon

Apple and Peanut Butter Slices

 2 minutes approx.
 1 or 2 children as a snack

Food you'll need
1 apple
peanut butter (smooth or crunchy,
    100% natural if possible)

How to make it

1 Chop the apple into slices, whatever way you like.
2 Spread with peanut butter and eat!

Ants on a Log

 5 minutes
 2 or 3 children as a snack

Food you'll need
2 sticks of celery
cream cheese (or peanut butter)
raisins

How to make it
1 Wash and dry the celery sticks.

2 Cut off the ends and tops and cut each celery stick into 3 pieces.
3 Using a teaspoon or a knife, spread cream cheese (or peanut butter) onto the celery.
4 Add the raisins on top.

Other quick and simple snacks

- A slice of cheese, an apple and a handful of popcorn
- 2 oatcakes with peanut butter, blueberries and a few chocolate chips
- Selection of raw veggies with hummus and fruit
- Handful of chopped nuts and a pear or other piece of fruit
- 2 dates stuffed with peanut butter and a sprinkle of coconut, and a small orange

Cool Cucumber Butterflies

These snacks are a cool thing to make if you're having some friends over. They will be very impressed with your cooking skills!

 10 minutes

 3–5 children as a starter or snack

Stuff you'll need
chopping board
child-safe knife
teaspoon
bowl

Food you'll need
1 cucumber
½ cup of hummus (see the recipe on
　page 43)
¼ pepper
about 20 pretzels

How to make it

 1 Wash and dry your cucumber. Cut both ends off and then chop the cucumber into 8–10 thick slices.

2 Using a teaspoon, scoop out the inside of each piece to create a space for the hummus, making sure not to go all the way through the cucumber.

3 Pop the scooped-out cucumber in a bowl and mix it with the hummus. Spoon it back into the holes in each piece of cucumber.

4 Slice the pepper very thinly and put two strips into the hummus kinda sticking out – these will be the antennae of the butterflies.

5 Stick a pretzel on either side of the hummus to make 'wings'. Et voilà – cucumber butterflies!

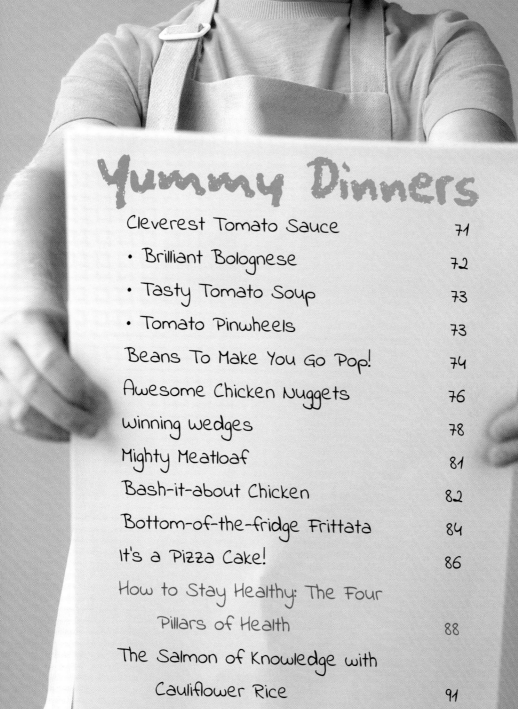

Yummy Dinners

Cleverest Tomato Sauce

This clever sauce will be your friend for life! You can use it to make lots of different dinners and snacks.

 about 10–15 minutes

 30–40 minutes

 3 children and 2 adults for 1 pasta dinner. Freeze any leftovers.

Stuff you'll need

child-safe peeler
chopping board
child-safe knife

large saucepan
wooden spoon
blender

Food you'll need

2 carrots
2 onions
3 or 4 sticks of celery
a splash of olive oil
3 cloves garlic
1 handful fresh basil leaves

1 tbsp balsamic vinegar
2 x 400g tinned tomatoes or 6 cups of
   fresh tomatoes when in season
large handful fresh spinach
salt and pepper

How to make it

1 Peel the carrots and the onions and chop into small dice (see page 13).
2 Dice the celery.
3 Heat the oil in the saucepan on a medium heat and then add all the veggies.
4 Cook gently, stirring everything with your wooden spoon.
5 Peel and chop the garlic nice and small.
6 Tear the basil leaves into smaller pieces.
7 When the veggies are soft (prod one with a knife to check), add the garlic, balsamic vinegar and basil.
8 Then add the two tins of tomatoes and stir everything well.
9 Fill an empty tin with water and use it if the sauce starts to get too thick.
10 Add some salt and pepper and then simmer for 30 minutes.
11 Add the spinach and cook for a further 2 minutes.

12 When your sauce is cooked, blend it to make it really smooth.

Serve with wholemeal pasta (cooked according to the instructions), or see pages 72–73 for more ideas.

Here are some of the things you can do with the Cleverest Tomato Sauce

HARD

Add some oil to a large saucepan over a medium heat and fry one chopped-up onion. Then add 400g mince and stir until the meat is all brown. Add a tablespoon of tomato puree and 3 cups of Cleverest Tomato Sauce and mix. Let it cook for around 20 minutes, stirring from time to time. Serve with wholemeal pasta (cooked according to the packet instructions).

Brilliant Bolognese

 5 minutes

 25 minutes

 3 children and 2 adults

Tasty Tomato Soup

 2 minutes

 5–10 minutes

3 children

To make this super-tasty soup, add 1 to 2 cups of chicken or vegetable stock to 3 to 4 cups of the Cleverest Tomato Sauce in a saucepan. Heat slowly, stirring all the time.

Tomato Pinwheels

 5 minutes

 15–20 minutes

 9–12 pinwheels

Preheat the oven to 200 degrees. Roll out a sheet of puff pastry, spread it with ¼ to ½ cup of the Cleverest Tomato Sauce and sprinkle with your toppings: mozzarella, chopped mushrooms, sweetcorn or whatever you fancy. Roll it up like a Swiss roll and cut it into thick slices. Lie them flat on a baking tray. Glaze with beaten egg and bake in the oven for 15–20 minutes. Great for a snack, lunchbox or an easy dinner!

Beans To Make You Go Pop!

What's with the funny name of this recipe? Well, did you ever hear the song: 'Beans, beans, good for your heart, the more you eat, the more you fart'? Yes, beans can make you go pop!

 5–10 minutes

 20–30 minutes

 3 children and 2 adults as a side dish

Stuff you'll need

chopping board

child-safe knife

large saucepan

measuring spoons

Food you'll need

1 medium onion

2 tbsp olive oil

2 cloves garlic

1–2 tbsp smoked paprika

1 tin chopped tomatoes

1 tbsp tomato puree

1 tin cannellini or haricot beans

salt and pepper

How to make it

1 Peel the onion and chop it into small dice.

2 Put the oil into the saucepan and turn on the heat to medium.

3 Add the chopped onion and cook slowly until the onion is opaque (see-through).

4 Peel and chop the garlic into tiny pieces. Add it, along with the smoked paprika, the tomatoes and the tomato puree, to the onion. Mix well.

5 Cook everything for 10–15 minutes. Keep stirring every few minutes and add some water if the sauce starts to stick.

6 Add the beans and cook for a further 5 minutes. Have a taste and add salt and pepper if you want.

> Eat with: toast, baked potato and cheese, Bash-it-about Chicken (see page 82), fried, boiled or scrambled egg (see page 24), or on their own – but keep all the windows open, just in case!

Awesome Chicken Nuggets

Chicken nuggets are really easy, a bit messy and fun to make!

 about 15 minutes   15–20 minutes   3 children and 2 adults

Stuff you'll need

2 baking trays
baking paper
blender
3 small bowls
measuring cups and spoons
chopping board
child-safe knife

Food you'll need

4 slices wholemeal bread
1 cup flour (any type)
1 tsp garlic powder
1 large or 2 small-to-medium eggs
4 free-range Irish chicken breasts
1 carrot and 1 pepper, cut into sticks,
    to serve

How to make it

Breadcrumbs

1 Turn the oven on to 200 degrees and line a baking tray with baking paper.
2 Tear your slices of bread into 4 and throw them in the blender.
 3 Blend the bread and when it is like sand, spread it evenly on the baking tray.
4 Pop it into the oven for 5–7 minutes to toast it, turning once. Remove from the oven when toasted and turn the oven down to 180 degrees.

Chicken nuggets

1 In the first bowl, put a cup of flour and the garlic powder. Mix them together.
2 In the second bowl, add your egg(s) and mix well.
3 In the third bowl, put your toasted breadcrumbs.
 4 Chop your chicken into two-bite-sized pieces.
5 Get the baking trays ready by lining them with baking paper.
6 Dip each piece of chicken first into the flour, then in the egg and finally into the breadcrumbs, making sure it's fully coated. Pop it onto your baking tray.
 7 When all the chicken is done, put the trays into the oven for 15–20 minutes. Turn them once after about 10 minutes.
 8 You'll know the nuggets are cooked when the meat is fully white.

Serve with your favourite dip and veggies for lunch or, if you're really starving, make some Winning Wedges too (see page 78).

Winning Wedges

These tasty wedges go great with Awesome Chicken Nuggets.

 about 15 minutes

 35–45 minutes, depending on the size of your potatoes

 3 children and 2 adults

Stuff you'll need

chopping board
child-safe knife
large bowl
1 or 2 baking trays
baking paper
measuring spoon

Food you'll need

4 or 5 large potatoes
2 tsp garlic powder
olive or rapeseed oil
salt and pepper

How to make it

1 Leaving the skins on, chop the potatoes in half, lengthways. Cut them in half again, lengthways, and then cut these quarters in half again. You should get 8 wedges out of each potato. If your potatoes are very large, cut them again. The wedges should all be roughly the same size.

2 Throw them into a large bowl. Cover them completely with hot water from the tap or kettle and let them soak for 15 or 20 minutes. (This removes the starch from the spuds and helps them to crisp up.)

3 Line 2 baking trays with baking paper and turn your oven on to 180 degrees.

4 When the soaking time is up, drain the potatoes and dry them completely in a tea towel.

5 Put them into a dry bowl and add the garlic powder, a couple of tablespoons of oil and some salt and pepper.

6 With your hands, mix everything well in the bowl. It'll be messy!

7 Place the wedges on the baking trays in neat rows – they shouldn't be on top of each other.

8 Pop them into the oven for about 35–45 minutes until they are golden brown and cooked all the way through – taste one to see (let it cool down first 'cos it will be hot, hot, hot!).

9 Serve with your favourite dipping sauce.

Mighty Meatloaf

This is simply meat made into a loaf like a loaf of bread!

 15–20 minutes   60–75 minutes   3 children and 2 adults

Stuff you'll need

chopping board
child-safe knife and peeler
frying pan

blender
large bowl
loaf tin

Food you'll need

1 brown onion
4 garlic cloves
3 carrots
3 sticks of celery
1 medium courgette
handful button mushrooms

2 tsp dried rosemary
2 tsp dried thyme
oil, salt and pepper
400g minced beef (1 medium pack)
1 egg, beaten
¼ cup grated cheddar cheese

How to make it

1 Turn the oven on to 180 degrees.
2 Peel the onion, garlic and carrots. Dice the onion and garlic.
3 Roughly chop the carrot, celery and courgette before blending for a few seconds.
   (No blender? No problem! Just dice all the veggies nice and small.)
4 Warm a tablespoon of oil on the frying pan and cook the onion gently.
5 Pop all your veggies and the garlic into the pan with the onion and stir well.
6 Add the rosemary and thyme and some salt and pepper.
7 Cook for 3 to 5 minutes until the veggies are soft, then take them off the heat.
8 While they are cooling, grease the loaf tin (see page 13 for how to grease a tin).
9 In your large bowl, mix the meat, egg and grated cheese together.
10 Add the veggie mixture to the meat and mix everything well.
11 Plop the mixture into the tin and press it down. Bake it in the oven for 60–75
   minutes. Stick a fork in and if it goes all the way through, that's a good sign
   that the meat is cooked.
12 Serve it in slices with mashed spuds, some steamed broccoli or a green salad.

Bash-it-about Chicken

If you've had a bad day at school or have had a row, then this is a great recipe to make! You can bash the chicken and that will help you feel better!

 about 5 minutes

 5–7 minutes

 3 children and 2 adults approx.

Stuff you'll need
baking paper
rolling pin (and muscles!)
frying pan
tongs
chopping board

Food you'll need
4 chicken breasts
olive oil
salt and pepper

How to make it
1 Place a chicken breast in the middle of a piece of baking paper and fold the paper over the chicken.
2 Take the rolling pin and bash the chicken to flatten it so that it's the same width all the way around and is about twice its original size.
3 Bash the rest of the chicken breasts as well.
4 Rub the chicken with oil on both sides and season with some salt and pepper.
 5 Add some oil to your frying pan and heat it to a medium to high heat.
6 Add the chicken breasts – you want to hear a sizzle when they go into the pan.
7 Cook the chicken on both sides for a couple of minutes. Use tongs to turn the pieces over. You might fit only one or two chicken breasts in the pan at a time.
 8 Pop the chicken onto a chopping board and cut into it to check that it is white all the way through. Chop it into slices – yum!

How to serve it
- In a burger bun with lettuce and tomato
- With pasta and Cleverest Tomato Sauce (see page 71)
- With mashed potatoes, coleslaw and broccoli
- Leftovers can be used in sandwiches or popped into lunchboxes.

Bottom-of-the-fridge Frittata

To make this dish, you can use more or less any veggies from the bottom drawer of your fridge or from your freezer.

 10 minutes   20–30 minutes   3 children and 2 adults

Stuff you'll need

small saucepan
chopping board
child-safe knife
large ovenproof frying pan

measuring cups
large bowl
whisk

Food you'll need

400g baby Irish potatoes
1 large onion
1 tbsp butter
2 cups chopped veg – whatever you
    have in the bottom of your fridge,
    e.g. pepper, mushroom, tomato,
    courgette, spinach, peas, sweetcorn

8 eggs
¼ cup milk
½ cup fresh herbs (basil, mint,
    oregano) or 2 tbsp dried mixed
    herbs
salt and pepper
¼ cup grated parmesan

How to make it

1 Half fill your saucepan with water, put it on the cooker and bring it to the boil.

2 Wash your spuds, chop them into quarters and pop them in the hot water.

3 Let them cook for 5 to 8 minutes. Use a sharp knife to check if they are cooked through. Don't let them go all mushy!

4 Cut the top and bottom off the onion and peel it. Chop into small dice.

5 In a large frying pan, heat the butter gently over a low heat and when it's melted, add the onions. Cook gently (low and slow) for about 5 minutes. (Don't let them burn. If they start to burn, turn the heat down and add a couple of teaspoons of water.)

6 While the onion is cooking, chop the rest of your veggies into small pieces.

7 Add them to the onions and mix well. Allow the veg to cook until soft (about 4–5 minutes).

8 Drain the potatoes and let them cool a bit.

9 Turn the oven on to 180 degrees.

10 In a large bowl, crack the eggs and whisk them well.

11 Add the milk and herbs and a little bit of salt and pepper.

12 When the veggies are cooked, add the spuds to the oven-safe frying pan and then slowly pour in the egg mixture.

13 Top with some fresh, grated parmesan. Cook for about 1 minute and then pop the whole frying pan into the hot oven.

14 Bake for about 10–15 minutes (the eggs will become puffy and rise up and there should be no runny egg left).

15 Remove from the oven and place it on a tablemat on the table. Serve it straight away with some salad and crusty bread.

It's a Pizza Cake!

This easy pizza base is gloopy, messy and fun! Pop the toppings into bowls on the table and let everyone choose their own.

 25 minutes

 15 minutes approx.

 3 children

Stuff you'll need

measuring cups
large bowl
several smaller bowls

chopping board
child-safe knife
baking tray and baking paper

Food you'll need

For the base

1 cup thick Greek yoghurt
1–1½ cups self-raising flour

For the sauce

¼–½ cup Cleverest Tomato Sauce (see
    page 71) or 1–2 tbsp tomato puree

Toppings

Sweetcorn, mushrooms, red onion, spinach, peppers, olives, cooked meat (like chicken or ham), pineapple, grated mozzarella, grated parmesan

How to make it

1 Measure out the Greek yoghurt and dump it into your bowl.

2 Measure out one cup of flour, add to the yoghurt and mix it with your hands – it's gonna be sticky! Add flour to your hands to stop the dough sticking!

3 Keep adding small amounts of flour until the yoghurt and flour come together in one ball of dough that comes away easily from the side of the bowl. You may need up to half a cup extra.

4 Chop and slice all your toppings. Put them in separate bowls so that everyone can choose their own toppings.

5 Turn the oven on to 220 degrees.

6 Line a baking tray with baking paper and sprinkle some flour on it.

7 Divide the dough in three. Put each piece onto the baking paper and smush it down. Shape it into a circle (or a square or triangle! Who says a pizza has to be round?) by pushing into it using your fingers or your knuckles (it will be too sticky to roll).

8 Top with sauce (not too much – spread it thinly) and then add as many toppings as you like.

 9 Finish with as much or as little cheese as you fancy and then pop it into your hot oven for 8–10 minutes until the crust is browned and the cheese is bubbling.

 Try these tasty toppings

- Ham, pineapple, sweetcorn and olives
- Pepper, onion, sweetcorn and spinach
- A little bit of everything!

How to Stay Healthy – The Four Pillars of Health

Sleep

Sleep is like magic! It helps our bodies to heal and recover from a busy day. Just like our tablets and computers need to be recharged, our bodies need to be recharged through sleep too. You'll be a cranky-pants without enough sleep so get to bed on time and let sleep do its thing.

Eat

We all love to eat! Food is the fuel that keeps our bodies going during the day. Eating the rainbow, drinking lots of water, eating with friends and family and choosing wholemeal whenever possible are all great ways to get the most fun and energy out of the food we eat.

TOP TIP

Turn off screens one hour before bed – this is a terrific bedtime routine.

TOP TIP

Get involved in food from growing to buying to exploring to cooking it. It's fun!

Our health doesn't rely on just one thing, like doing lots of exercise or eating veggies; all four of these pillars keep us strong, well and happy!

Move

Not only is exercise good fun but it also helps to keep our bodies strong and flexible.
It helps us if we're feeling grumpy and it makes us tired so that we sleep better. There are hundreds of ways we can exercise: play tag, climb trees, football, gymnastics, swim, or bounce on your trampoline!

Connect

If we get stressed or feel sad this might affect our overall health. When you feel like this, it's important to talk to someone you trust – a parent or your teacher – so they can help you. If you find it hard to talk about your feelings, try drawing a picture to explain how you feel.

TOP TIP

Our bodies are designed for moving so try walking or cycling instead of going everywhere in the car!

TOP TIP

Spend time in nature or with your friends when you're feeling sad.

The Salmon of Knowledge with Cauliflower Rice

Have you ever heard of cauliflower rice before? It's kinda like rice except it's made out of cauliflower so it's not really rice at all!

 15–20 minutes and 1 hour to marinate

 15 minutes total

 3 children and 2 adults

Stuff you'll need

bowl

measuring spoons

teaspoon

grater

large knife

ovenproof dish

chopping board

blender

frying pan or wok

Food you'll need

Salmon

1 tbsp honey

1 tbsp soy sauce

2 tbsp olive oil

1 inch (3 cm) root ginger

2 garlic cloves, peeled

4 fillets salmon

1–2 tbsp sesame seeds

Cauliflower Rice

1 head of cauliflower

olive oil

1 cup frozen peas

How to make it

Salmon

1 Put the honey, soy sauce and olive oil in a bowl.

2 Scrape the skin off the ginger with a teaspoon and grate it (use the smallest hole on your grater).

 3 Chop the top and bottom off the garlic cloves and chop them really small or use a garlic crusher.

4 Add the ginger and garlic to the bowl and mix well with the other ingredients.

5 Pop your salmon into an ovenproof dish and pour the sauce over it.

6 Put it into the fridge for an hour and run outside to play, go to GAA or finish your homework.

7 Once the hour is up you can turn the oven on to 180 degrees.

 8 Sprinkle the sesame seeds on top of the salmon and slide it into the hot oven. While it's cooking (this will take 10–12 minutes), make the cauliflower rice.

Cauliflower rice

 1 Chop the leaves off the cauliflower and break or chop the head into pieces (florets).

2 Put half the pieces into the blender and blitz until it looks like rice. Empty the blender and then do the other half. You might have to stop and start the blender to move larger pieces of cauliflower around so that it all gets blended nicely.

 3 In a large frying pan or wok, heat some oil on a medium heat.

4 Tip the 'rice' into the pan and stir gently.

5 Add the peas and mix well.

6 Cook for 2–3 minutes. Add some water if it starts to stick – a tablespoon at a time.

7 Check on the salmon in the oven after 10 minutes. To check that it's cooked, cut into the thickest piece to make sure it's light pink all the way through.

8 When the rice and salmon are cooked, place some of the 'rice' on a plate and top with the lovely salmon.

9 Sprinkle some extra sesame seeds on top to decorate it. Mmm!

Cool Food Fun!

Have you heard the legend of Fionn mac Cumhaill who tasted the Salmon of Knowledge and gained all the world's knowledge, becoming the greatest of all men in Ireland? If you eat lots of salmon, it will help keep your brain working really well (might just help with those spelling and maths tests!)

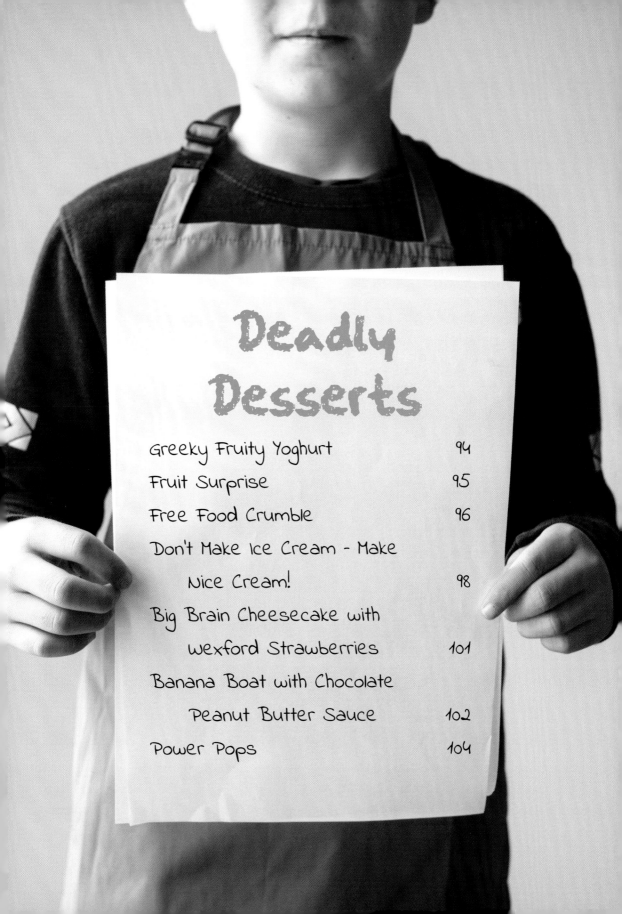

Deadly
Desserts

Greeky Fruity Yoghurt	94
Fruit Surprise	95
Free Food Crumble	96
Don't Make Ice Cream - Make	
Nice Cream!	98
Big Brain Cheesecake with	
Wexford Strawberries	101
Banana Boat with Chocolate	
Peanut Butter Sauce	102
Power Pops	104

Greeky Fruity Yoghurt

This is really easy to make. Try different fruits and nuts to change it up each time.

🎨 5–10 minutes

🍽️ 1 child (just multiply ingredients for more people)

Stuff you'll need

chopping board
child-safe knife
measuring spoons
small bowl
fancy bowls to serve

Food you'll need

fresh fruit like apple, orange, pear, berries, banana, pineapple, kiwi and melon (about 1 cup per person)
2–3 tbsp Greek yoghurt
2 tsp honey
toasted flaked almonds or chopped nuts of choice (see page 27 for how to toast nuts)

How to make it

1 Chop all the fruit into bite-sized pieces.
2 Mix the yoghurt and honey in a small bowl.
3 Divide the fruit between the bowls.
4 Top with the honey and yoghurt mixture and sprinkle some toasted nuts on top – delicious!

Fruit Surprise

This is a great first dessert for little ones to make from the age of 3+. Everyone will love the 'surprise'!

 5 minutes

🍽 3 children

Stuff you'll need

3 bowls
measuring cups
chopping board
child-safe knife

Food you'll need

small handful chocolate chips
3 cups fresh fruit of choice e.g. orange,
   banana, kiwi, grapes
1–2 tbsp toasted chopped nuts and
   seeds of choice (see page 27 for how
   to toast nuts and seeds)

How to make it

1 Place the chocolate chips at the very bottom of three bowls.

 2 Chop the fruit into small pieces.

3 Place the fruit, nuts and seeds on top of the chocolate chips.

4 And surprise! When you get to the bottom of your bowl, you'll find your chocolate chips!

Free Food Crumble

It's fun to go blackberry picking in the autumn and you can make this lovely, warming dessert with your free blackberry treasure!

 5–10 minutes

 30 minutes approx.

🍴 3 children and 2 adults

Stuff you'll need

chopping board
child-safe peeler
child-safe knife
small saucepan
wooden spoon

mixing bowl
small bowl
spoon
8-inch (20-cm) baking dish

Food you'll need

For the fruit

6–8 eating apples (any type)
4 tbsp pure maple syrup
2 tsp vanilla extract
2 tsp cinnamon
2 tsp ground ginger
2 cups blackberries (fresh or frozen)

For the crumble

¼ cup plain wholemeal flour
1 cup oats
¼ cup sunflower seeds
½ cup nuts (walnuts, almonds,
   hazelnuts work well)
2 tbsp pure maple syrup
2 tbsp olive oil

How to make it

1 Peel and chop the apples into small dice and throw the core into your compost bin.

2 Into the saucepan, put the apples and 2–3 tablespoons of water, the maple syrup, vanilla, cinnamon and ginger.

3 Turn on the heat to medium and cook your apples. Use a wooden spoon to break down the apples as they soften.

4 After about 5–8 minutes, add the blackberries.

5 Mix well. If the mixture starts to stick, add a little extra water. Cook for another 3–5 minutes or so until the fruit is soft.

6 Pour it into the greased baking dish and get on with the topping!

7 Turn the oven on to 180 degrees.

8 Pop your flour and oats into a mixing bowl.

9 Roughly chop the sunflower seeds and nuts and add them to the bowl.

10 Mix the maple syrup and olive oil together in a small bowl and pour it in with the flour and oats.

11 Time to get your hands messy! Mix everything well with your fingers.

12 Tip the mixture on top of the fruit mixture and flatten it down.

13 Bake for 20–25 minutes until the top is nicely browned and the filling is bubbling.

14 Serve with crème fraîche and toasted almonds or Nice Cream (see page 98).

Don't Make Ice Cream – Make Nice Cream!

Nice cream is like ice cream but is made with bananas! It is super easy to make and you can add lots of other ingredients!

 5 minutes and then another 5–10 minutes when frozen

 2–24 hours

 3 children and 2 adults

Stuff you'll need

chopping board
child-safe knife
freezer bag
blender

Food you'll need

4 ripe bananas
½ cup of milk

How to make it

 1 Chop the bananas into chunks and pop them into the freezer bag.

2 Freeze for at least two hours or, even better, overnight.

 3 Put the frozen banana chunks into your blender and blend!

4 The frozen bananas will go crumbly first and then gooey.

5 Stop the blender and scrape down the sides from time to time.

6 Add a little bit of milk as required (but not too much) to loosen the bananas.

7 Keep blending until the bananas start to have the consistency of creamy, soft-serve ice cream (almost like a 99!).

8 Eat immediately with your favourite toppings or put into an airtight container and freeze for a couple of hours to make a harder 'nice cream'.

Try these tasty options

You can make lots of variations. Add your flavours towards the end of blending:

- Chocolate Nice Cream – add 2 tbsp cacao powder and ¼ cup walnuts
- Strawberry Nice Cream – add ½ cup chopped strawberries
- Everything Nice Cream – add 2 tbsp cacao powder, ½ cup chopped strawberries, 1 tbsp peanut butter and a handful of chocolate chips

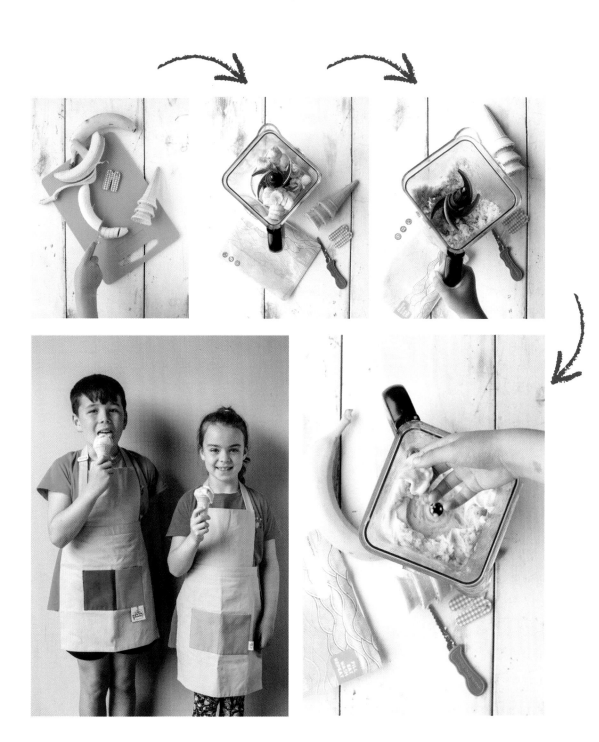

Big Brain Cheesecake with Wexford Strawberries

This dessert is really easy to make and requires no baking. It's especially nice with wexford strawberries on top!

 15 minutes   2–3 hours   3 children and 3 adults

Stuff you'll need

measuring cups and spoons
blender

5–6 individual ramekins or 8-inch (20cm) pie dish

Food you'll need

For the crust

1 cup pitted dates (dates with no stones)
1 cup mixed nuts (walnuts, almonds, cashews)
3 tbsp cacao powder
2 tbsp desiccated coconut
2 tbsp coconut oil, melted

For the filling

1 cup cream cheese (a full 200g pack)
1 cup Greek yoghurt (full-fat)
$1/3$ cup maple syrup
2 tbsp cacao powder
1 tsp vanilla extract
handful dark chocolate chips
Wexford strawberries to decorate

How to make it

Crust

1 Pop the dates, mixed nuts, cacao powder, coconut and melted coconut oil into a blender and blitz till the mixture comes together into a ball like dough.
2 Divide this between each of the six dishes and smush it down until it's flat. Or pop it into the pie dish and, using the back of a spoon, press it down into the dish.
3 Put this in the fridge while you make the filling. Wash your blender!

Filling

1 Blend all the ingredients for the filling (except the chocolate chips and strawberries) for a couple of minutes until everything forms a nice creamy mixture. Add the chocolate chips and mix through the filling.
2 Spoon on top of the base and put in the fridge for a couple of hours.
3 Just before serving, decorate with some sliced strawberries. Yum!

Banana Boat with Chocolate Peanut Butter Sauce

A delicious, quick and easy dessert to make!

 5 minutes   1 (just multiply ingredients for more people)

Stuff you'll need
chopping board
child-safe knife

plate
measuring cups and spoons

Food you'll need (per person)
1 ripe (but not brown) banana
½ cup plain yoghurt
1 tsp vanilla extract
½ cup fresh berries

small handful toasted chopped nuts
    and seeds (see page 27 for how to
    toast nuts and seeds)
1 tbsp chocolate chips
1–2 tsp chocolate peanut butter sauce
    (see below)

How to make it

1 Chop the banana in half lengthways and sit it on the plate (like a kinda boat!).
2 Mix the yoghurt and vanilla together, and spoon it over the banana.
3 Throw fresh berries, toasted nuts and seeds and chocolate chips on top.
4 Drizzle with 1–2 teaspoons chocolate peanut butter sauce.
5 Eat immediately!

Chocolate Peanut Butter Sauce

  about 10 minutes   1 cup

Stuff you'll need
measuring cups and spoons
small saucepan
wooden spoon

Food you'll need
½ cup dark chocolate chips
2 tbsp peanut butter
½ cup milk of choice

How to make it
1 Put all the ingredients into the saucepan over a low heat.

2 Warm slowly, stirring all the time, until all the chocolate has melted and combined with the other ingredients. Perfect on the banana boat, on Nice Cream or drizzled on porridge!

Power Pops

These power ice pops will give you the energy to play and cook and do cartwheels and have fun!

 5 minutes   overnight   3 children

Stuff you'll need

measuring cups and spoons
blender
ice pop moulds
chopping board
child-safe knife

How to make it

1 Blend everything in your blender.
2 Pop into your ice pop moulds and freeze overnight.

Chocopop

2 tbsp raw cacao
1 cup milk of choice
1 large ripe banana
1 tbsp peanut butter

Tropical Treat

1 cup frozen mango
1 cup coconut milk
1 cup spinach leaves
½ ripe banana
1 tsp vanilla extract

Strawberries and Cream

1 cup Wexford strawberries, washed
1 cup Greek yoghurt
1 tsp maple syrup
2 tsp chia seeds

Celebration Time

St Patrick's Day

St Patrick's Day is celebrated on 17 March every year. St Patrick is one of our national saints, as I'm sure you know. Celebrate by trying to eat as many green foods as you can!

Pancakes Glas Blasta

These are perfect for breakfast on St Patrick's Day, before you head to the parade. And they have spinach in them to give you lots of power for the day ahead!

 5 minutes

 5 minutes approx.

 3 large or 6 small pancakes

Stuff you'll need

measuring cups and spoons
blender
frying pan

ladle or large spoon
plates

Food you'll need

1 cup flour (wholewheat or spelt or whatever you have)
1 cup milk of choice
1 cup spinach leaves
2 eggs
1 tbsp butter, melted

1 tsp baking powder
½ tsp bicarbonate of soda (bread soda)
olive oil for frying
mandarin orange segments and crème fraîche to serve

How to make it

 1 Pop the flour, milk, spinach, eggs, melted butter, baking powder and bicarbonate of soda into a blender and blitz them until you have a smooth, green mixture.

 2 Turn your oven on to 120 degrees.

3 Pour some oil onto the frying pan over a medium heat and gently heat it up.

4 Add a ladle/spoonful of the pancake mixture to the pan and cook for a couple of minutes.

 5 Flip over and cook on the other side. Slide it onto a plate and pop it into your warm oven while you cook the rest.

6 When all the pancakes are cooked, divide them between three plates. Top them with mandarin orange segments and crème fraîche to look like the Irish flag. Go hálainn!

Paddy's Day Soup

Try this easy, tasty, minty green soup for lunch!

 15 minutes

 15–20 minutes

🍽 3 children and 2 adults

Stuff you'll need

chopping board

child-safe knife

large saucepan

measuring jug

blender

Food you'll need

1 medium onion

1 tbsp olive oil

1 tbsp butter

½ head of broccoli

1 clove garlic

5 cups frozen peas

2 chicken or vegetable stock cubes

handful fresh mint

salt and pepper

How to make it

 1 Chop the onion in half and peel off the skin. Dice it nice and small.

2 Add the oil and butter to the saucepan and warm them up over medium heat.

3 When the butter is melted, add the onion and cook it for about 5 minutes, stirring every now and again, until it's opaque (almost see-through).

 4 While the onion is cooking, chop the broccoli up into small pieces.

5 When the onion is done, add the broccoli and mix well. Cook for a couple of minutes. Add a little bit of water if it starts to stick.

 6 Peel the garlic and chop it up nice and small. Add it to the saucepan.

7 Pop the kettle on. Meanwhile, bung the frozen peas into the saucepan and stir.

 8 Crumble the stock cubes into the pot and add 1 litre of hot water from the kettle and stir well.

9 Tear up most of the mint leaves and add them to the saucepan and then let everything simmer for about 10 minutes.

 10 When the broccoli is cooked, take the saucepan off the heat. Very carefully, taste the soup and add salt and pepper if needed.

 11 If it's too thick, add more water. Then pour it into your blender and blitz until it's completely smooth. Top your soup with the rest of the mint leaves – yum!

Easter

'Spring' into the kitchen to make these great Easter recipes!

Eggcellent Easter Muffins

These muffins are full of tasty carrots and a perfect Easter treat.

 15–20 minutes   15 minutes or so   makes about 16 muffins

Stuff you'll need

muffin cases
muffin trays x 2
large bowl
chopping board
child-safe knife
peeler

grater
small bowl x 2
fork or whisk
measuring cups and spoons
wooden spoon
cooling rack

Food you'll need

1¾ cups (200g) self-raising flour
   (wholemeal if possible)
1½ tsp baking powder
½ tsp bicarbonate of soda (bread soda)
½ tsp salt
½ tsp ground ginger
1 tsp ground cinnamon
1 tsp vanilla extract

3 large or 5 small–medium carrots
½ cup walnuts plus extra for
   decorating
1 cup raisins
$1/3$ cup coconut oil
½ cup maple syrup or honey
1 cup plain Greek yoghurt
2 eggs

For the icing

½ cup cream cheese
½ cup Greek yoghurt

1–2 tbsp maple syrup
1 tsp vanilla extract

How to make it

1 Turn on your oven to 180 degrees.
2 Pop the muffin cases into the trays.

3 In a large bowl, put the flour, baking powder, bicarbonate of soda, salt, ginger, cinnamon and vanilla and mix everything well.

4 Cut the tops and bottoms off your carrots and peel them. Grate them into the large bowl (see our grating tip on page 9).

5 Roughly chop the walnuts and add them and the raisins to the bowl.

6 Melt the coconut oil in the microwave (it takes 30 seconds to a minute). Add it, the maple syrup or honey and the Greek yoghurt to the bowl and stir well.

7 Crack the eggs into a small bowl (see tip on page 12), whisk them and add to the big bowl and mix.

8 Now you're ready to divide the mixture between the muffin cases. Use a spoon or an ice cream scoop to do this.

9 Pop them into your heated oven for 15 minutes.

10 Carefully remove from the oven and cool them on a cooling rack.

Icing

1 To make the icing, combine all the ingredients in a small bowl and mix well.

2 Keep the icing in the fridge until the muffins are cooled down and you are ready to eat them. Ice only the ones you are going to eat straight away (because the icing has yoghurt in it).

3 Top with chopped walnuts – delish!

Leftover Easter Egg Cookies

This is a great way to use up leftover Easter eggs. These cookies can even be eaten as a quick breakfast - how cool is that?!

 10 minutes

 15 minutes or so

 makes 12–14 cookies

Stuff you'll need

plate	baking paper
fork	small bowl
large bowl	chopping board
baking tray	child-safe knife

Food you'll need

2 medium-sized ripe bananas	1 tbsp maple syrup
2 cups oats	½ cup chopped nuts
2 tbsp coconut oil	½ Easter egg or handful choc chips

How to make it

1 Turn the oven on to 180 degrees.

2 Peel the bananas and mash them really well on a plate, using a fork.

3 Put them into a large bowl, add the oats and mix.

 4 Melt the coconut oil in the microwave for 30 seconds to a minute. Add the oil, the maple syrup and the chopped nuts to the large bowl. Mix like a mad thing!

5 Smash your Easter egg half into small pieces, if using.

6 Pop some baking paper onto a baking tray.

7 Scoop spoonfuls of the mixture onto the tray and shape them into cookies using your hands or the back of the spoon.

8 Pop some pieces of Easter egg or chocolate chips on top of each cookie.

9 Bung them into the oven for 15 minutes – they should be golden and delicious when cooked.

 10 Carefully remove them from the oven and let them cool down before you scoff them!

Halloween

Here's some fun food to make for your Halloween party or to add to your lunchbox at Halloween!

Scary Sweet Potatoes

These are an excellent snack to eat before you head out trick-or-treating or to have for your dinner on Halloween night!
You can make the faces look scary or friendly.

 10 minutes

 10–15 minutes

 3 children (as a snack)

Stuff you'll need

chopping board
child-safe knife
paring knife

bowl
baking tray
baking paper

Food you'll need

1 or 2 thin sweet potatoes
1 tbsp olive oil

1 tsp smoked paprika
ketchup for dipping

How to make it

1 Turn the oven on to 180 degrees.

2 Wash and dry the sweet potatoes but don't peel them.

 3 Slice them into thin, round slices – these are the faces!

4 Using your paring knife, cut out small triangles for eyes and a mouth from each slice.

5 Mix the olive oil and smoked paprika in a bowl, and toss the slices in the mixture.

6 Pop some baking paper onto your tray.

7 Place the faces onto the tray, making sure they are not on top of each other.

8 Bake for 10–15 minutes until soft.

9 Carefully remove them from the oven. Serve them straight away with ketchup blood, and maybe add mayonnaise to make a spider's web!

Chocolate Apple Mummies

These are really fun to make. You can use up any chocolate you get in your trick-or-treat bags!

🎨 45 minutes (including 20 minutes to set and 10 minutes to decorate)

🍴 Makes 4–6 portions approx.

Stuff you'll need
chopping board
child-safe knife
measuring cups
lollipop sticks
saucepan and bowl or 2 bowls
baking tray
baking paper
spoon

Food you'll need
2 large apples
2 cups of 70% chocolate chips or
    chocolate (400g) plus about 20
    more dark chocolate chips
1 cup white chocolate chips or white
    chocolate (200g)

How to make it
1 Wash the apples and dry them really well (or else the chocolate won't stick).
 2 Cut them into thick slices width-wise.
3 Break up the chocolate and melt it in the microwave or 'bain-marie' (see page 14).
4 Make a small slit in each slice of apple at the bottom and push the lollipop stick into it.
5 Place some baking paper on the baking tray.
6 Dip the apple slices into the melted chocolate – you might need to use a spoon to help make sure they are fully covered.
7 Pop the apple slices onto the baking tray and put it into the fridge for about 20 minutes.
 8 Melt the white chocolate in the same way you melted the dark chocolate.
9 Take the apples from the fridge. Using a spoon, drizzle the white chocolate back and forth across the apple slices so it looks like mummy bandages!
10 Carefully drip two small circles for eyes and top them with dark chocolate chips.
11 Let them set again and serve them to all your friends.

Seasonal Eating

What does eating 'in season' mean?

Fruits and veg grow at different times of the year or season. Eating 'in season' means eating those foods that are ripe and ready to be picked or dug up at the correct time.

Why is this important?

There are a number of reasons:

- It is better for the environment. For example, if we want to eat something that is out of season in Ireland, like strawberries in January, then they have to come here from another country. And that's a lot of air miles just so you can have strawberries on your porridge in January!
- Food tastes better when it is in season because it is fresher and perfectly ripe. If your strawberry has to come from overseas, it will be picked before it's ripe so that it doesn't go off while travelling. It will be stored in a fridge for a long time and this will also affect the flavour.
- Food keeps more of its nutrition when it's eaten in season. Your strawberry might lose some of its health powers if it has been on an airplane for a long time!
- It's cheaper to eat in season because the farmer will have lots of the food he or she has grown and may want to sell it quickly before it goes bad.

Cool Food Facts

- Did you know that some foods grow all year around like lettuce, cauliflower and cabbage?
- And that strawberries are the only fruit that have their seeds on the outside?
- Did you know that our bodies can't break up the outside husk of the sweetcorn? You might see it again in the toilet bowl!
- Did you know that potatoes have different names like Rooster and Kerr's Pink? See what you can find in the supermarket.

Spring: February, March, April

- Carrots
- Cauliflower
- Leeks
- Lettuce
- Mint
- Mushrooms
- Rhubarb
- Spinach

Summer: May, June, July

- Asparagus
- Aubergine
- Berries
- Courgette
- Cucumber
- French beans
- New potatoes
- Peppers
- Spring onions
- Tomatoes

Autumn: August, September, October

- Apples
- Beetroot
- Berries like blackberries
- Broccoli
- Onions
- Pumpkin
- Sweetcorn
- Turnip

Winter: November, December, January

- Artichoke
- Beetroot
- Brussels sprouts
- Carrots
- Celery
- Garlic
- Kale
- Turnip

Christmas

Hands up if you love Christmas! Here are some cool things you can make at this time of year.

Toy Show Hot Chocolate

This tasty hot chocolate is great to sip while watching The Late Late Toy Show or your favourite Christmas film.

- 5 minutes
- 3 children

Stuff you'll need
measuring cups and spoons
small saucepan
whisk
wooden spoon
3 mugs

Food you'll need
2 cups milk of choice
¼ cup maple syrup
1 tbsp cacao powder
1 tsp vanilla extract

How to make it

Option 1
1 Put all the ingredients into a small saucepan.
2 Turn on the heat to low and warm gently.
3 Whisk everything as it warms up.
4 Don't let it boil as it will be too hot.
5 Pour into mugs and enjoy!

Option 2
1 Divide the cacao between 3 microwave-safe mugs.
2 Add a small drop of milk to each cup and mix well.
3 Divide the rest of the milk between the mugs and pop them in the microwave for 1 minute.
4 Take out and stir well. Add a teaspoonful of maple syrup to each mug and a ½ teaspoonful of vanilla extract.
5 Mix again and return to the microwave for another 30 seconds to 1 minute (depending on your microwave).

EASY

Christmas Chocolate Bark

 15 minutes   about 30 minutes   3 children

Stuff you'll need

2 baking trays and baking paper

saucepan

a bowl that fits into the saucepan

Food you'll need

½ cup flaked almonds

½ cup desiccated coconut

1 cup (200g) dark chocolate (70% cocoa)

How to make it

1 Turn your oven on to 180 degrees.

2 Put some baking paper onto one tray and scatter the flaked almonds onto it. Make sure they are well spread out.

3 Pop the tray into the oven for about 3 minutes.

 4 Take the tray out and add the coconut. Make sure everything is well spread out. Toast in the oven for another 3–4 minutes. Be careful though, as it can burn very easily.

 5 While you're waiting for the nuts and coconut to toast, break up the chocolate and melt it, using the microwave or 'bain-marie' method (see page 14).

6 Lay some baking paper onto the second tray.

7 Pour the melted chocolate onto the second tray. Tilt the tray this way and that to spread out the chocolate into a nice thin layer.

 8 Take the nuts and coconut out of the oven – they should be a nice tan colour and smell delicious – and let them cool slightly.

9 Before the chocolate is set, grab handfuls of the nut and coconut mix and scatter it all over the chocolate. Make sure that every piece of coconut and almond comes into contact with the chocolate or it will just fall off.

10 Pop it into the fridge for 30 minutes to set.

11 When it's hard, take it off the tray and just snap it into pieces. Enjoy!

> ### Cool Food Tip
> This makes a great gift for your best friend, or your Granny or Grandad. Break the bark into pieces, pop them into a festive box or jar and decorate with ribbon!

Index

About the author

Deirdre Doyle is a health coach and a mum of three. She has educated thousands of children about food and cooking through her award-winning business, The Cool Food School, since 2018. Her focus is on making food fun for kids.

 thecoolfoodschool.ie

thecoolfoodschool

thecoolfoodschool

@coolfoodschool